I0473850

The Reluctant Lawyer

Transitioning From One World to the Next

ALBERT R. HARTLEY

Copyright © 2012 by Albert R. Hartley

Published by *AlbertRHartley.com*
636 CEDAR ROAD
CHESAPEAKE, VA 23322
www.AlbertRHartley.com

ISBN-13:978-1477483169
ISBN-10: 1477483160

No part of this publication may be reproduced, stored in a retrieval system or transmitted in any form or by any means, electronic, mechanical, photocopying, recording, scanning, or otherwise except as permitted under Section 107 or 108 of the 1976 United States Copyright Act, without either the prior written permission of the publisher, or authorization through payment of the appropriate per-copy fee to Albert R. Harley, 636 Cedar Road; Chesapeake, VA 23322. Requests can be submitted via mail or email to Albert@AlbertRHartley.com.

Limit of Liability/Disclaimer of Warranty: While the publisher and author have used their best efforts in preparing this book, they make no representations or warranties with respect to the accuracy or completeness of the contents of this book and specifically disclaim any implied warranties of merchantability or fitness for a particular purpose. No warranty may be created or extended by sales representatives or written sales materials. The advice and strategies contained herein may not be suitable for your situation. You should consult with a professional where appropriate. Neither the publisher nor the author shall be liable for any loss of profit or any other commercial damages, including but not limited to special, incidental, consequential, or other damages.

Readers should be aware that Internet Web sites offered as citations and/or sources for further information may have changed or disappeared between the time this was written and when it is read.

AlbertRHartley.com is a fee-based service that helps individuals and small businesses to achieve their full potential through personal and private, one-on-one coaching sessions and via an online video training library.

Layout and Cover Design by Melissa Powers and T.D. Wright Enterprises.
www.TDWrightEnterprises.com

This book is dedicated to Amy

Some History, So You Know My Bias...

I grew up in an upper middle-class environment with good parents who worked hard. Lawyers, doctors and engineers were venerated and placed into a fantasy world I would never enter. Access was limited with entry granted to those in higher education. I lacked the guide to navigate easily and quietly through this uncharted territory. It was difficult to resist yielding to my natural reaction to be cautious or halt in my pursuit.

I was not familiar with educated, powerful people in my youth. Middle-class to poor, middle-class people made me feel comfortable in my own skin. The most they ever wanted to know was whether or not I saw 'the game' last night. Rich, educated people want to compare curriculum vitae to size you up because they are fearful that you are going to take something away from them. I never experienced this attitude of scarcity until I went to college with rich, prep school kids. Initial introductions with these individuals did not produce standard conversational language, but rather tongues of interrogation to see how quickly I could be outclassed, out-educated and ostracized. This created my biggest fear entering law school: *Am I good enough?*

The landed gentry have little need to worry about this. If they fail they have a back up plan that rarely depends on their own creation. If only I was so lucky. As I struggled to get through college and fit into my new social surroundings, I longed for the easy conversations of the hard-working men and women that I cherished in my youth. Determination and blissful ignorance fueled my passion and efforts to stand at the gate of the fantasy world of higher education. Little did I know that once I pushed through those gates I would be transformed forever. Leaving behind a world of predictable consistency, I reluctantly walked into the world of hidden danger. I am The Reluctant Lawyer.

Naivety...

Law school teaches you that The Law is the only light needed for any and all issues obscured in darkness. While this was true for me to some extent, the moment I reviewed a contract and spoke to a client for the first time was when I realized the light of The Law was not enough. I attended enough business meetings with my father to avoid blindly swallowing the idea that academic knowledge was sufficient. I was unaware that there was a drastic chasm between the halls of law school and the practice of law. My belief was that once I got my bar license I would enter a world filled with educated people working towards the same goal. The realization that my 100k education and mountain of debt had not prepared me for the world of law was at once both harsh and depressing. Naiveté kicked my butt. I am a lawyer... now what?

I had four appointments on my first day that I set up before I was licensed. With a valued education I ignored my lack of experience and gave it a shot. Translating my knowledge into tangible powers should be a snap, right? WRONG! I was blown away by how little law school helped me practice law.

Dressed in my fresh suit and ready to unleash my

knowledge onto the world, I was suddenly confronted with my woeful insufficiency. Not only was I presented with my client's legal and financial problems, but they brought emotional and spiritual issues into my office as well. When did I become a pastor, mentor and confidant? Sure, knowing what the specific legal issue a client brought forth was pretty easy to identify and finding the solution was not impossible, but the other "stuff" was outright overwhelming. A person who passes the bar has the basic knowledge to pick a problem and throw something at it from the books. It's like the old saying, "Even a blind squirrel gets a nut now and then." I thought all lawyers were the same. I mean, we all have the same training, right? WRONG AGAIN!

So allow me to enlighten you and list the reasons why I hate lawyers. Yes, I am a lawyer, which may or may not make me a sellout of sorts. However, my list highlights general observations compiled over a twelve-year career of working, communicating and fighting with lawyers. In the case of the truest rules in life, exceptions do exist. In fact, I am a friend to many of those exceptions and I consider them to be some of the finest attorneys and finest people in the world. They know who they are and will not be offended by this list. So here goes:

1. The only professionals condemned by Jesus were lawyers.
2. Most of them create more problems than they solve.
3. They are selfish people.

4. They refuse to stop seeing angles of leverage at every turn.
5. They are not trustworthy. Information is a weapon to them so the more you give them the stronger they are.
6. They are overly concerned about the way they are perceived by people.
7. The truth is pliable.
8. Justice does not enter into their thought process.

So what is the point of this book? It sounds like I am a bitter, cynical jerk who is unaware of himself. While this is all true, I genuinely love practicing law. It is a privilege to help people with their life, both good and bad. This book is a cautionary tale to people who think that they can change the world, or want to try, but realize that the task is beyond them. It is also a guide to moving from old worlds to new. How do you keep up the fight without losing everything you believe in and what you want out of your life?

WARNING: You have to make a choice when given the following options:

- Right or Money
- Freedom or Oppression
- Joy or Depression
- Hope or Cynicism
- Principle or Principal
- Compassion or Indifference

If you make the correct choice you may keep your sanity but be prepared to be very lonely.

Which brings me to my next list...

Simple warnings from The Reluctant Lawyer to anyone who will interact and engage with human beings:

Listening

1. What?? I did not HEAR you!
2. Say no to more than drugs.
3. "Danger, Will Robinson!"
4. Please snack on these saltine crackers while I ignore your request for a glass of water.
5. Shut up and listen!

Fight

1. Avoid saddling that horse!
2. Stick to your guns.
3. A.H. stands for more than my name.
4. Learn to fight another day!
5. Tap out!

Self-Awareness

1. Is that the sound of your own drummer?
2. Don't hang out with your own kind.
3. Keep your friends close and fear closer.
4. Apologize and ask for forgiveness.
5. There is always a fool in the room. If you don't know who it is find a mirror.
6. I represent the enemy!
7. People suck.

Logistics

1. "Gett'n after it!"
2. Don't dive in the shallow end.
3. 2 + 2 = Rainbow
4. Know where to park your butt.
5. Network, network, network…
6. Hesitation is death.
7. You CAN handle the truth.
8. Tebow it.

ALBERT R. HARTLEY

Listening

ALBERT R. HARTLEY

What?? I Did Not HEAR You!

The success rate of any interaction can be traced back to how well the people in a given conversation listen. You are thinking, "Duh... I paid for this?" This might seem obvious to you, but think again. I am not simply referring to what you are *hearing*. Listening is *hearing beyond the words*. Listening is the process of using words to unearth or reveal the truth that a person is afraid to outwardly convey.

People in pain or in trouble rarely lead with their fear, pain or trouble. Poignant transparency is rare when people are hurt, scared or wounded. Don't expect immediate trust, you need to build trust through empathy. If law school does not beat it out of you, compassion might be warranted in certain circumstances. When the person is talking to you in an initial interview or confrontation, the assumption is that what they are saying is what you should listen. WRONG! What they are saying gives you the clues as to what questions to ask.

If the person is concerned about their finances, for example, they might start out with a narrative about how another party took money from them or how they paid another party a sum of money. Listen closely to the statements about money and formulate some questions.

Ask, "Has this put you in a financial strain?" Notice two things about this question:

1. It places the responsibility of this financial strain on someone else.
2. It is a yes or no question that requires a definitive answer.

If you only hear the narration about the "crook" that stole the money then you might think that the issue is getting the money back when in fact the issue is that this person is in a financial strain and they need help. Further, they don't have the money to pay anyone to help them get the money back. If you focus on "getting the money back" then you will follow their disguised path and realize too late that this client does not have the financial stamina to run the course. Conflict will arise and your relationship will inevitably sour.

Listening should be active. With one statement you should hear three things at once. I call this Ninja Listening. Here is a way to look at the listening process.

1. I hear the words that you say – White Belt

2. I hear the words and realize they are cluing me into something else you are not verbally communicating – Purple Belt

3. I hear the words, I process the clues and now I am asking questions that have you reveal your intimate fears and allow me to craft proper solutions – Congratulations, you are now a black-belted Ninja Listener.

If you truly wish to develop this skill, it is best to shadow a Ninja Listener to emulate their listening abilities. Write down the questions they ask. Typically the questions a Ninja asks are not in response to the raw information presented. It will look like the Ninja is not listening to the person at first glance, however, another Ninja would identify the three levels of listening. Training yourself to be a Ninja Listener will make you a better professional, a better father, husband, mother, wife, son, daughter and a better person overall.

ALBERT R. HARTLEY

14

Say No To More Than Drugs

Being eager to help or solve someone's problem ignores a fundamental fact: Not everyone can be helped. Some people feed off the drama of a problem in order to create scenarios that keep them in crisis. Learning to define the scope of the transaction requires a definitive NO.

Do not fall under the spell of surrender. Trigger words that will let you know that you are getting sucked in are "what if" statements or "let's try another approach first" and so on. This language is manipulative and detrimental to your sanity.

IF YOU FEEL A NO COMING ON THEN GO FOR IT. SAY NO, TELL THEM THANK YOU AND END THE MEETING!

ALBERT R. HARTLEY

"Danger, Will Robinson!"

Language is power. If you are struggling for clarity with someone you give that person leverage and make yourself vulnerable. The other person might say something like, "That is not what I heard you say" or "Are you sure that is what you said?" This is a trap. "Danger, Will Robinson!" You have someone who only wants to hear what they select to hear! Because it is impractical to write down every word you say you have to be direct.

It is best to follow a simple formula. Prior to stating a very difficult thing for someone to hear you should clearly say aloud, "I am going to say something very directly to you that is difficult to hear. Are you prepared to hear it?"

Ask them if you need to repeat it and then wait for them to speak next. Never speak after you have hit someone between the eyes with information. Read their body language and see if their shoulders slump or sit back. These gestures are a sign of submission. If they move the conversation to something else then they have rejected your statement. Submission to the statement would be followed by something like, "I understand" or "I am not sure I understand what you are saying." Either way, they are listening to what you have to tell them. Another way to move them towards submission is to ask them to repeat what you said and then ask, "Do you have any questions about the consequences of what I told you?"

My conference room is set up with a large white board that I use to write statements that need emphasis and clarity. Once you eliminate the person's ability to move away from the truth, you are forcing them to submit to the truth and follow your lead. The rest of the relationship you will be in the driver's seat. After writing this I see how horrible this sounds but the reality is that if you are trying to accomplish something for someone he or she has to be in the backseat. You drive, they follow. It still sounds horrible but I think I will leave it being horrible but accurate.

Please Snack On These Saltine Crackers While I Ignore Your Request For A Glass Of Water

Chances are pretty good that you have attended a social event in which you find yourself surrounded by more strangers than friends. In an attempt to make conversation, you sit down with someone and bring up a pretty mundane subject. The other person stares blankly for a minute until they interrupt you with something completely off topic. In an instant, you feel dismissed and undervalued. Put the same situation in the context of a professional setting and you are downright ticked off. Not only were you ignored but you also paid the person for it.

Professionals are typically trained to hear a problem, not a person, so they typically appear insensitive, aloof and arrogant. Rarely is this the intended effect but the client's perception takes precedence. Keeping the main issue or topic at hand is the most important aspect of opening a professional dialogue. If someone comes into my office about a will, I don't initially start making jokes about someone "kicking the bucket" or "buying the farm." Don't get me wrong, I am not above these jokes, but the goal of the initial meeting is to create common ground so sensitivity to my surroundings is crucial. Aggressive interactions with potential clients from the beginning keep the tensions high throughout the relationship. Luckily there are some simple rules you can follow to assess a person's needs accurately and sensitively.

Use direct language. Be polite but provide direct answers to a question. If someone is under a tremendous pressure regardless of what it is they need definitive parameters. As Jesus said, "Let your yes be your yes and your no be your no."

Remove distractions surrounding the main issue. Make sure that you eliminate other issues that are not crucial to the problem at hand. I find it helpful to list the issues on a piece of paper and get the client to agree that the list is accurate and complete. Once they see all the issues, you can prioritize the issues so that you focus on the most important ones.

Resist talking over the client. I am horrible about interrupting people because I am often thinking quicker than my memory can handle. Make a note on a piece of paper and make sure to ask them if they are finished before you proceed.

Remember: If the client or person wants a drink of water don't feed them saltines.

Shut Up And Listen!

Solving the problems of others is a high calling that takes a lot of hard work. There are times, however, when people simply need you to sit down and listen to them. The self-declared "problem-solvers" of the world easily fall into the trap of focusing on the problem rather than the person. Resist the need to immediately solve a seemingly identifiable problem. Some people need to be listened to and nothing else. Don't charge them if you are not actively doing something for them. Build an ally and believer of your system instead of counting every second. That simple investment will return huge dividends, in business and in life.

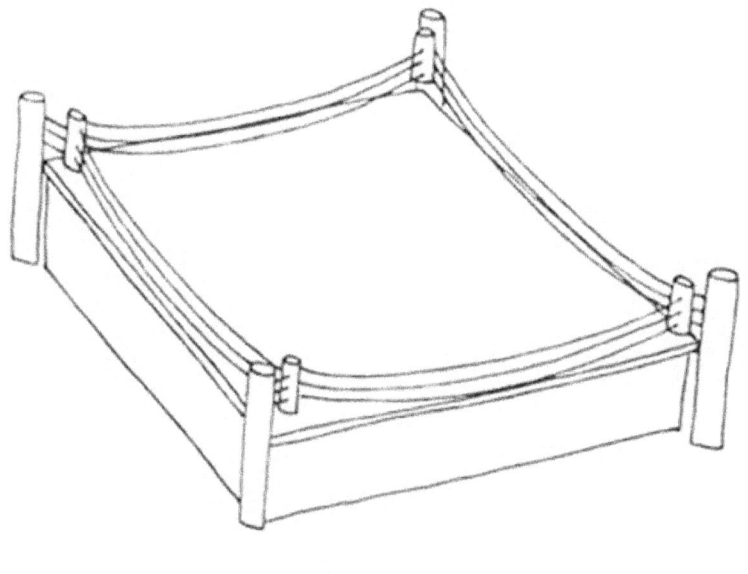

Fight

ALBERT R. HARTLEY

Avoid Saddling That Horse

A conclusion that rocked my world when I started practicing law was the need for human beings to have control in any given situation. Freedom from rules and the opportunity to declare, "You're not the boss of me" drives people to spend money and suffer. Consequently, it makes a lot of lawyers rich.

A person will fight to the death to teach someone that they are in control. Divorces are driven by this idea. People will pay a life of wealth to lawyers everyday to ensure that someone else loses while ignoring the clear truth that no one will win in the end.

Throughout my career I discovered that imposing anything on someone leads to sabotage and pain. Forcing someone to accept responsibility is going to get you a little bit of whatever you want but it won't get you anything you need. In order to get what you need you have to create a situation in which a person does what you want but believes it is their idea. If you create a scenario that leaves someone with a lack of freedom or control, they will find a new route to gain it back. Often this is achieved through the sabotage of your original plan.

Control is crucial. No one gives it up without a fight. They allow you to initially dominate them so that they can get away from your overbearing presence. Then they begin plotting their revenge against you for oppressing their freedom and control. Never lead a client to water and think that they won't find a way to pee on your carpet.

Stick To Your Guns

Conformity kills creativity. If you want to be successful then you must walk to the beat of a different drummer. Hear your own music and work to share your uniqueness with the rest of the world. Don't fold like a cheap house of cards as soon as someone criticizes your actions or ideas. Defend your position, hold fast to your convictions and push a little. Rolling over at the first sign of resistance means you are weak and insincere. Pouting if you don't win, however, is also bad form. Let it go. When you can't fight anymore don't become a jerk. Concede and be part of the team. Never say I told you so.

A.H. Stands For More Than My Name

A part of sticking to your guns is risking being disliked and openly criticized. I can be argumentative and inflexible when I think I am right, which is always, so I am not very gracious. My wife once told me that my initials stood for more than my name, which was a not-so-subtle way of referring to me as a part of the human anatomy. Sometimes holding your position with stubborn determination will encourage those with less conviction to give up. You might be alone, but you will be able to run the race to the end.

Learn To Fight Another Day!

Getting voted down and conceding your position does not necessarily mean you give up the fight all together. Learn to fight another day by requesting that the opposing party fighting you review the situation at a later date. You also might be able to set a condition after the review by stating, "Look, I can see I am going to have to concede my position but I would like to get a commitment to review this issue again in a week. If _____ occurs then we can agree to do _____."

Winning a series of little meaningless battles might be a great way to boost your ego but it does nothing to sustain your position. Waiting for your moment to fight another day allows your resources to be replenished so that you can engage the enemy at full force.

Tap Out!

Popular martial arts fights end when one opponent gives up or "taps out." Tapping the other person on their arm or shoulder signifies giving up and admitting defeat. People often fail to tap out when they are already beat. There is no shame in losing or acknowledging the futility of an exercise. Seth Godin has written a great book about quitting called *The Dip*, which I strongly recommend everyone read. He discusses when and why to quit.

While I believe that it is important to know when and why to quit, I also believe it is as equally important to look for the learning moment in every interaction, especially quitting.

Let's look at some responsible statements:

- "That situation provided opportunities that I misread."

- "I did not prepare for that part of the meeting so I could be proficient."

- "The other side was better capitalized to take advantage of the market."

Compare the following:

- "I could have prepared if that person would have told me about that fact."

- "The accountant failed to provide me with the right information so I could not see that coming."

The last two sentences deal with other people and focus on how someone else failed to give the proper effort. Excuses and tapping out are not the same thing. Tapping out is extinguishing all of your possible efforts to achieve a goal and still falling short. Excuses blame others for your failure. Accept your failure by humbly tapping out and make an even bigger effort the next time.

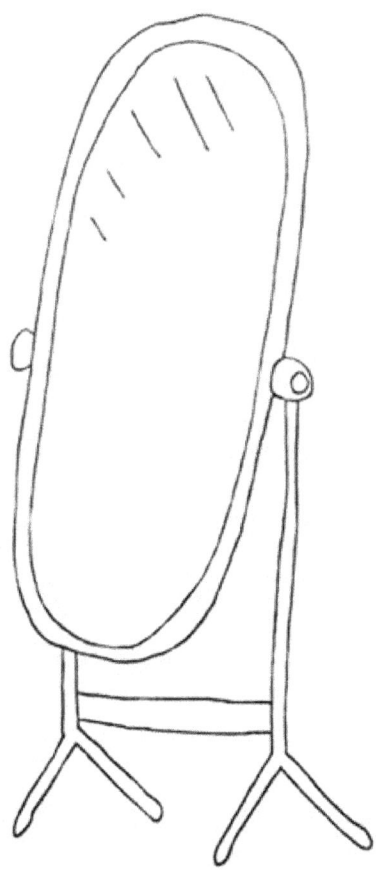

Self Awareness

Is That The Sound Of Your Own Drummer?

Supporters and detractors will always play a role in every aspect of your life, business and personal. Do well to avoid both when you need to push to another level. Each will tell you what they think you want to hear due to their equally intense love or hate for you. When things get tough ignore the outsiders. Turn inwards and seek the inner voice that yells out, "Sacrifice! Push! Don't give up!"

Don't Hang Out With Your Own Kind

Variety is the spice of life so mix it up as often as possible. Professionals love to insulate themselves with other professionals. Lawyers want everyone to believe that they are members of a superior club with restricted access. The simple truth is that no one willingly chooses to hang out with them. When you hang out with other people from various walks of life, occupations and backgrounds you are able to gather alternative perspectives. Refreshing your perspective is like refreshing your webpage. The site is updated and new items can be seen clearly.

ALBERT R. HARTLEY

Keep Your Friends Close and Fear Closer

One of the most powerful emotions is fear. It is often viewed in a negative way and seen as an emotion one needs to avoid in order to be successful. While fear can easily keep you away from a lot of things that you need and want, it can also help you to avoid a lot of poor decisions and mistakes. Identifying fear and confirming that it is not out of your current equation allows you to move forward and avoid mistakes. Some people will tell you that fear is an emotion that should be eliminated but I strongly disagree. Know it, understand it and use fear to your advantage.

Apologize and Ask For Forgiveness

OK, you screwed something up! Now what do you do? The answer is simple: Apologize and ask for forgiveness.

Many opportunities come out of success, but the transformation of a failure into a successful situation is pure magic. A simple formula for a successful apology works 99 percent of the time: Call the person on the phone or meet with them in person. DO NOT EMAIL THEM. Emails are for informing someone not communicating with them. Do not underestimate the power of a face-to-face interaction or phone call in repairing a relationship with a simple, "I am sorry, please forgive me. This is what I did and I won't do it again." You gain more business and create better relationships as a result of sincere apologies.

Remember that apologies do not always fully repair your network. More often then not, scars and rough patches remain that create friction and barriers to future interactions. Apologies help bandage the issue and ease some of the pain, allowing for new interactions to occur later down the road.

ALBERT R. HARTLEY

44

There Is Always A Fool In The Room. If You Don't Know Who It Is, Find A Mirror

In large meetings everyone thinks about their position in the room. Think about the last meeting you were in. Did someone strike you as an idiot? Did he or she get what they wanted? Yes? Then does that make the individual a powerful idiot?

Every meeting you enter is a Survivor episode with strategic planning. If the meeting is going in a direction you want don't grandstand or show boat. A professional meeting is not the time or the place. Sit quietly and inwardly celebrate your success. If the meeting is going in a direction you don't want, change the direction if possible and get out of the way to allow the bandwagon to move toward the goal. Momentum is important in meetings.

Never talk too much. Say what you need to say and sit down. If you have been given 10 minutes use seven. The more you talk the more likely you will make a mistake. If you are sitting in a room and thinking, "I am not going to get credit for something," stop! You are the idiot. It is best to refrain from talking. Unless you are a valuable contributor to conversation, stay silent.

ALBERT R. HARTLEY

I Represent The Enemy!

Realizing that the person you represent may be the very person you should be watching out for is an important revelation. Typically, the best way to forge a great client relationship is to set the expectation of the client from the initial meeting. You have to confirm, using the other techniques in this book, that the client has accepted a range of possibilities. Don't forget that the client is under stress and pressure to fix a difficult problem.

Think about an animal attack. Siegfried and Roy roamed freely with their lions and never expected the animals to attack. Roy forgot that his "friend" or "pet" was a natural predator and one day he attacked, leaving Roy physically scarred. Like the instinctual tiger, clients turn against me and attack. Acting on instinct, they blame me for their unfortunate circumstances. Like Roy, I have failed to recall that a client was the enemy and allowed them to attack.

Documenting and covering your backside must be a parallel goal for handling people in stressful situations. They will seem fine one day and lunge at you like a tiger the next. Follow your protocol, don't make exceptions and never think that verbally informing someone is enough.

Communication and, most importantly, paperwork are the best defenses against a client turning against you.

People Suck

News flash for the hopeful, sunshine spreaders in the world: I have seen people at their worst and know that people suck. We are at our worst when human beings are hurt, scared or pressured. The hugely selfish and frightened human being is incapable of doing a good thing without defiling it with something bad in unfortunate conditions.

Never assume that your client, staff or even your friends will do the right thing. This is a rarity. Be overwhelmed when they do the right thing but never be disappointed that they do the wrong thing. It is always a good idea to hope for the best but never forget to plan for the worst because people suck.

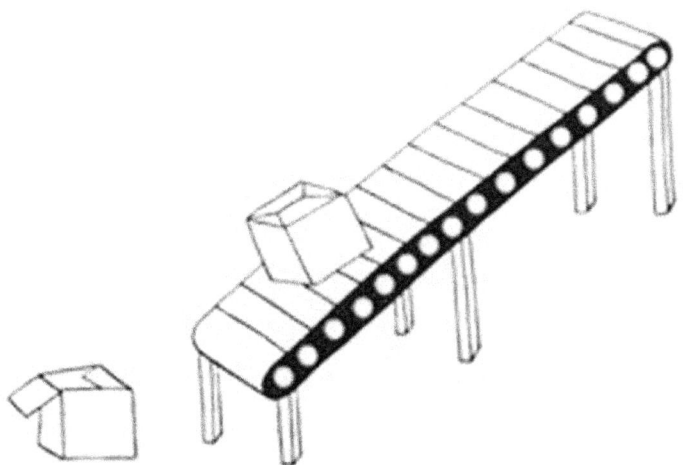

Logistics

ALBERT R. HARTLEY

"Gett'n After It!"

I don't want to be on old fart here but people are shocked to discover that great work requires hard work. Nothing worth gaining comes to you instantaneously. The work needed to go from good to great is partly due to getting a head start. Showing up is three-fourths of the battle so getting where you are supposed to be before everyone else is crucial. It is just as important as being the last to leave. I am not advocating anyone to ignore other, possibly equally important responsibilities in order to be first. What I am advocating is something my dad referred to as "gett'n after it."

"Gett'n after it" is the focused determination that you will work earlier and later than everyone else if that is what it takes to be successful. If someone asks why you are there so soon tell them you that you are "gett'n after it." If you are truly passionate about your work you should start early, leave late and get after it!

ALBERT R. HARTLEY

54

Don't Dive In the Shallow End

Take a second to clear your mind and picture a piece of paper and an aquarium. The differences are pretty clear. The paper is flat and two-dimensional. The aquarium, on the other hand, has the ability to hold things that are multi-dimensional and allows for each side to interact differently with the other items floating around.

Most business is thought of as a linear equation. Similar to the piece of paper, it is often viewed as flat and static. Realistically the power of any business relationship, whether legal or another type, is the dynamic interaction of the various parts. Your network should be vertical not linear.

The linear network does not create reciprocity necessary for self-generating referrals. Linear networks tend to look like production lines, which require someone to input the material at one end so that "the product" is processed at the other end. One way in and one way out.

A vertical network is dynamic. Vertical networks create synergy amongst the various parts that begin to feed off one another so all parts are self-generating referrals. Vertical networks develop a give and take pushing each piece, whether it is left, right, top, down or center, toward multidimensional energy. Stop looking for one-to-one connections and seek out persons with multiple connections that can generate business for you when that original connection is paused.

2 + 2 = *Rainbow*

A life of patterns is not reversed in one meeting. Be careful assuming that a legal solution can solve a spiritual or emotional problem. Typically the spiritual and emotional problems exist prior to legal counsel. However, legal problems usually include emotional and spiritual troubles as well, so coming up with the right antidote to counteract the effects of years of stupid choices is one of the reasons a lawyer's hourly rate is $250 per hour and up.

The complex subtlety of a situation requires the artist's focus not the technician's single-mindedness. Lawyers think that a legal solution will fix everything. Take divorce for example. Lawyers can always do divorce work because it is so prevalent. Every marriage begins and ends with a legal transaction but that is not what causes the conflict.

Divorce lawyers ride in on the white horse selling their services to desperate people looking for any answer because they are miserable. Soon the lawyer is the problem because the person does not know what they need they just know what they want. The client transfers problems that have nothing to do with the law into the lawyer-client relationship. Their selfishness or contempt for others creates a vortex lawyers slip into. The lawyer gets branded a betrayer or incompetent as soon as he or she does not produce what they want. Avoiding this vortex starts with setting the client's expectations about the good and the bad. Never just mention the gain. Always focus the client on the negative or risk leaving the upside to a time that will surprise them.

Science includes formulas that produce predictable outcomes. The art of solving a problem is found in the race against time and new information. You don't have time to scrap your hypothesis and start the experiment over. Jackson Pollack started with the same materials almost every time he painted but I am pretty sure that he never ended with the same painting twice.

Know Where to Park Your Butt

Someone much smarter than me has probably already waxed eloquent notes on where to sit in a room. I worked on this because I am neurotic. Most of my physical placement in a room or at a table deals with my fears and anxiety of not being in control of my surroundings. So in case you are as neurotic as I am, here are some tips:

Always sit to push the reason for the meeting. In other words, if you want a decision to be made before the conclusion of the meeting, then sit with your back to the exit door and place anyone else on the opposite side of the room. This creates the illusion that the only way an exit can be made is through a decision, ideally a decision in your favor. You are the gatekeeper and if they want to get out of the room, figuratively speaking, then they are forced to agree with you. The idea that you are sitting in front of freedom reinforces the need for them to agree to your position. If you create a path to exit for them they will run through the door like animals to a slaughter.

Ask someone to move seats if you are not comfortable with where they are sitting. Note: Only do this if you are hosting the meeting. Otherwise, you risk offending someone or everyone.

To ensure that they sit at the place you want, set up a pen and paper at one particular seat. For complete assurance that the other person will not relocate, provide them with a form to fill out at the desired seat, presenting them with an obligation and lack of choice.

Network, Network, Network...

I believe "network" is an overused misnomer in our culture. When people use the word "network" they talk about arriving early to cocktail hour to "network." Twitter, Blogger and Facebook are all forms of popular "social networking" as well. So what does this word really mean?

Networks provide connections to share information. So in a sense, Facebook is an outlet for that. However, business networks need to define focus. Business networks focus on the decreased cost of business and increased profitability. A network is a collection of relationships developed for solving problems in areas so someone else can come into your sphere of influence. Facebook friends and other online acquaintances are not networks. A network feeds you and you feed it. The network that you build should be self-sustaining by the give and take of referrals from all sources that connect with you.

ALBERT R. HARTLEY

Hesitation Is Death

Consensus is great and committees have their function in certain cases but concrete decisions hold the power. Even if you are unsure what the perfect solution is, make a decision and ride it out long enough to see if it is working. Immediate results only happen at McDonald's and they can still get your order wrong. Be patient when you have made a decision and avoid looking back until the process related to the decision is completed.

Once it is completed decide if it is working or not. If not, kill it by making another decision. Don't linger like you are at a wake. Assess the situation, process the data and listen to your gut. Then decide and implement your decision. Be tough and make the change. If you don't, someone or something else will make the decision for you. Hesitation is death.

You CAN Handle the Truth

The film *A Few Good Men* is based on a lawyer from the same are where I practice. He is a very nice gentleman, but I digress. The scene where Tom Cruise demands the truth and Jack Nicholson screams, "You can't handle the truth!" is ridiculously famous and also true. Most people can't handle the truth and, therefore, fail to ask the right questions.

I am always struck by people who will waltz around a question hoping that I will let them off the hook and offer the information so that don't have to ask for it. One of the most awkward questions in a divorce case that you are required to ask in Virginia is when was the last time sexual relations occurred between spouses. Since couples have to be separated for a certain period without having sexual relations before they can divorce in Virginia, the question has to be asked. AWKWARD! The first time I ever approached this question I asked, "When was the last time you two were, uh, together?" The husband simply answered, "We just had lunch today without our kids." Smooth, right?

Here is some insight. Most people can handle the truth. What they can't handle is a lie that obscures the truth. As a lawyer, I regularly am forced to give out bad news, even devastating news on occasion. I believe that you can approach people respectfully and honestly to deliver truth and it will be received. Pandering to people and dismissing the pain around a topic does nothing to help them and only reflects poorly on you. Maybe this doesn't apply to everyone and you can't handle the truth.

Tebow It

Everyone has heard that first impressions are the most important. While there is a lot of truth to this statement, I believe that last impressions make all the difference. People remember the last interaction more than the first impression. You could have a difficult first interaction, maybe you failed to set expectations or the facts turned out to be different than you thought, but you may be offered a chance to change that impression. Evaluate and reset the expectations so that the last time you see the person or do business with the person they leave thinking that you "finished well." Leaving a good final impression is crucial to building the vertical network and referrals that all contacts should lead.

Finishing well also embodies another principle that I want to leave as the last take away from this book: Forever improvement, or what the Japanese refer to as "Kaizen." This is absolutely crucial to success. Never settle or believe that a product, process or service is perfected. Always improve and always look for ways to finish well.

Think about what significant interactions require a finish-well style: a good night kiss, a beautiful eulogy, an incredible graduation speech, or a Hail Mary pass. These are the images that overshadow the rest of the transaction. Doug Flutie's Hail Mary pass is replayed over and over in the world of sports. It takes mere seconds but no one really remembers the other 60 minutes of the game. I am not suggesting that the entire process can be a hot mess and you pull a rabbit out of your hat at the very end. I am suggesting that great work is determined by the final minutes of a transaction if they are reviewed and altered accordingly. That is when a good process can become a great experience.

A Closing Thought ...

So now that you have reached the end, take this simple idea away from this book: You are going to make mistakes and screw things up. That is a fact of life but you can choose to focus on how mistakes are corrected. Do what it takes to finish well.

Thanks,

Albert R. Hartley, The Reluctant Lawyer

ALBERT R. HARTLEY

About the Author...

Albert R. Hartley runs his own law firm, The Hartley Law Group, P.C., where he works as a real estate attorney. He resides in Chesapeake, Virginia with his loving wife, Amy, and two daughters. Albert graduated from The College of William and Mary and received his law degree from Regent University. Visit his blog at www.AlbertRHartley.com to learn more about successful strategies for today's changing world.

www.ingramcontent.com/pod-product-compliance
Lightning Source LLC
Chambersburg PA
CBHW071621170526
45166CB00003B/1140